THEN & NOW

SPORT

NIGEL SMITH

FRANKLIN WATTS
LONDON • SYDNEY

An Aladdin Book
© Aladdin Books Ltd
1996

*Designed and
produced by*
Aladdin Books Ltd
28 Percy Street
London W1P 0LD

ISBN 0 7496 2468 X

*First published in
Great Britain in 1996
by*
Watts Books
96 Leonard Street
London EC2A 4RH

The author, Nigel
Smith, is a teacher and
the author of many
history and
information books for
young people.

Consultant
Chris Harte, secretary
of the Association of
Sports Historians

Editor
Katie Roden

Design

David West
CHILDREN'S BOOK DESIGN

Designer
Flick Killerby

Picture Research
Brooks Krikler
Research

Illustrator
James Field – Simon
Girling & Associates

Printed in Belgium
All rights reserved

A CIP catalogue entry
for this book is
available from the
British Library

CONTENTS

INTRODUCTION	3
SOCCER	4
AMERICAN FOOTBALL	6
RUGBY	7
BASKETBALL	8
BATS AND BALLS	10
RACKETS AND BALLS	12
GOLF	14
WINTER SPORTS	16
WATER AND SPORT	18
HUMAN STRENGTH	20
ANIMALS AND SPORT	22
FIELD EVENTS	24
TRACK EVENTS	26
THE SPIRIT OF THE OLYMPICS	27
CYCLE SPORTS	28
COMBINED EVENTS	29
GAZETTEER	30
INDEX	32

INTRODUCTION

Sport is as ancient as the human race itself. Since the earliest times, people have competed against one another, in running, riding and other feats of human strength and endurance. The first Olympic Games took place in 776 BC, in Olympia, Greece. Then they were a demonstration of athletic skill; now they are the world's most important sporting contest. This book describes the origins and development of many of today's most popular sports and competitions.

Most people play sport simply as a leisure activity. A lucky few can earn their living as professional sportspeople. Some of the world's richest, most famous people are sports players, while many young players dream of winning an Olympic medal or playing for their countries. Sport is for everyone; there is no one who cannot take part in at least some of the sports mentioned in this book.

Sportspeople now use the latest technology and training techniques, from materials used in the NASA space programme to special clothing to increase their speed. New sports, such as snowboarding, are being invented all the time. But people's reasons for taking part in sports have stayed mostly the same since those very first Olympics – to enjoy themselves, to get fit, to perform to their best ability and to play fairly.

SOCCER

Soccer, or Association Football, is the most popular sport in the world. Kicking a ball has been a leisure activity for centuries; today, millions of soccer fans follow their favourite teams and top players are highly paid sporting heroes.

The ancient Chinese played football with a stuffed leather ball, over 2,000 years ago. They called the game *Tsu-Chu-Tsu*, or "to kick the leather ball with the feet". At about the same time, the Romans also played several football-type games. *Paganica* was a free-for-all competition, in which two teams rushed for the ball. In another game, *Harpastum*, the ball was simply grabbed and carried over the goal line.

THE GREATEST GOAL OF ALL
Since 1930, the world's top football teams have battled with each other to win the ultimate soccer trophy, the World Cup *(above)*. The championship is played every four years, each time hosted by a different country. The first competition was won by Uruguay.

HOLD ONTO YOUR HEADS!
Various forms of football were found among ancient peoples. Victories on the battlefield were celebrated in some cultures by kicking around the heads of enemy warriors! This grisly practice is thought to have begun among the Danish invaders of Britain, but it was most widely recorded by the ancient Chinese.

FROM MOBS TO MONEY-MAKERS

Football in medieval Britain was a violent sport with no rules. "Mob football" *(right)* was played by big groups of people, often in busy streets. In 1314, it was banned, but it was still played in many towns.

During the late 1800s, football developed into the game as we know it today. Rules were drawn up at English schools and universities and football clubs were formed over the years. Soccer soon became an organised sport and players began to be paid.

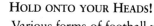

Aluminium studs

WHAT A CROWD!
Important soccer matches have always attracted enormous crowds... but none has beaten the Brazil versus Uruguay game in the 1950 World Cup. An amazing 199,589 people packed into the Maracaña Municipal Stadium in Rio de Janeiro, Brazil, to cheer on the two teams!

THE MODERN GAME

Today, soccer for both men and women has a massive following worldwide, and huge amounts of money are poured into the game. Clubs pay vast sums to buy top players – in 1995, a transfer fee for England's Andy Cole cost £8 million; Alf Common, in 1902, was sold for £1,000! Sponsorship of contests is a huge money-spinner, especially as televised matches offer worldwide advertising. Twenty-four countries now compete in the World Cup finals, with many more taking part in the qualifying matches beforehand.

Pelé

PELÉ
(b. 1940) *Pelé (Edson Arantes do Nascimento) is one of soccer's greatest players. During his career (1955-77), he scored 1,281 goals and helped Brazil to win the World Cup 3 times. He is now involved in Brazilian sports policy and training.*

FANCY FOOTWORK
Nineteenth-century leather boots weighed three times as much as modern ones. The new "Predator" boot *(below)* has streamlining cuts in the toe, which give a kick more force and control.

DRESSING UP
Early players wore tight trousers or breeches. Baggy, knee-length shorts were later introduced for freer movement.

1950s

These shorts became shorter and shorter over the years. Modern players wear close-fitting shirts and shorts, which display a sponsor's name.

SPEED AND SAFETY
Studs prevent slipping and are changed to suit the pitch.

Rubber studs

WHATEVER THE WEATHER
Some matches are played on pitches of artificial grass. Astro Turf was developed in the 1960s for the Houston Astrodome, an indoor stadium in the USA. It is made of plastic and fibres and players need to wear special boots *(right)* to play on it.

PLAYING BY THE RULES
The first referees were students from upper-class English families. They helped the team captains at Oxford and Cambridge Universities to draw up the rules of modern soccer in the nineteenth century. Today, referees make sure that the players act fairly and stick to the rules. A yellow card is shown as a warning to anyone who breaks the rules; a red card is shown for a serious offence and the player is sent from the pitch.

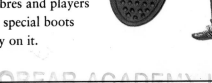

AMERICAN FOOTBALL

Early American football was originally based on rugby *(see page 7)*. During the nineteenth century, American students had played a wild, soccer-like game. It was so rough that some colleges banned their students from playing, so they began to develop American football, which was thought to be less dangerous.

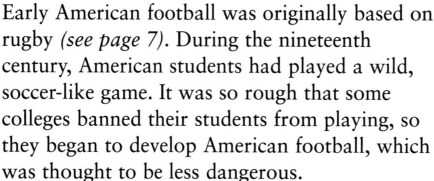

PADDING AND PROTECTION

Preparing for a game is like preparing for a battle! The body must be well protected, but the player must be able to move easily. Players protect their hands with gloves or tape and their bodies with armoured padding *(above)*. But many get injured; most players' careers last under ten years.

HEADGEAR

American football involves a great deal of physical contact and players have good head protection. They wear a strong, brightly coloured helmet *(above)*. Early helmets were made of leather; modern ones are made of tough, lightweight plastic. Team names usually suggest that the players are fearless warriors.

THE DEADLY GAME

In the early days of American football, there were few rules. The game grew so violent that in 1905, eighteen players were killed and 159 injured. President Theodore Roosevelt demanded that it should be made safer and new rules were introduced. These rules, as well as carefully designed protective clothing, mean that the game today is much safer.

WARPAINT

Some American football players wear coloured "warpaint" on their faces. As well as making them look fierce, it is also very practical. "Paint" is worn on the cheeks by people playing under floodlights. It stops reflections from their face affecting their eyesight. Thick sun-protection cream is worn on the nose and lips, to protect them during daytime matches.

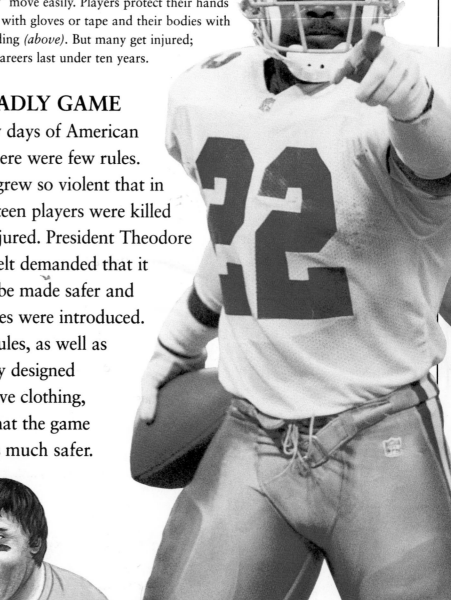

RUGBY

Legend says that rugby was invented in 1823 when William Webb Ellis of Rugby School, England, picked up a soccer ball and ran with it. In fact, it began when "hacking" (vicious tackling) was banned from soccer at the school and became the basis for rugby. Today, the game is divided into two types. In 1871, 17 amateur teams formed the English Rugby Union, followed by Scotland, Ireland and Wales. 21 teams left the English Union in 1895, as they wanted to pay their players, and formed the Northern Rugby Union (now the Rugby Football League), with different rules. Rugby Union became a professional sport in 1995.

WORLD CONTESTS
Rugby Union and Rugby League have separate World Cups. The greatest teams are New Zealand, France, Australia and South Africa.

Lomu

JONAH LOMU
(b. 1975) *Lomu was the star of the 1995 Rugby Union World Cup, scoring a record 7 tries for New Zealand. Several American football teams tried to sign him up. He also holds records in shot, sprinting, hurdles and discus.*

THE KIT
Players wear mouthguards on their teeth *(below)* and tape to protect their ears *(left)*. Some wear sticky strips to hold their nostrils open and let them breathe more easily.

A VIOLENT HISTORY!

In 1871, the Rugby Union set rules that banned "tripping, hacking and scragging (grabbing players by the neck)" so players had to invent less dangerous ways of stopping the player who had the ball. They now tackle by grabbing his or her legs *(below)*. The scrum, in which the opposing players push against one another in a struggle for the ball, can be very rough.

THE IRISH GAME
Gaelic football, which is played in Ireland, is a mixture of rugby and soccer. However, it is much older than rugby, dating at least from 1712. The ball is similar to a soccer ball, but it may be kicked, punched or "handpassed" (held in one hand and hit with the other). Gaelic football was taken to Australia by settlers and was developed into Australian Rules football in the 1860s.

7

BASKETBALL

One thousand years ago, the Maya and Aztecs of Central America played a ball game called *Pot-ta-Pok* (Mayan, *below*) or *tlatchi* (Aztec) as part of a religious ceremony. The object of the game was to shoot a solid rubber ball through a ring high on a wall. The winners received gifts from the spectators, but the losing captain was often beheaded. Basketball is a little like this grisly game – but no one loses their head! It is one of the USA's major sports and is played all over the world, but it is only just over 100 years old.

HUMBLE ORIGINS

James Naismith, a priest in Massachusetts, USA, invented basketball in 1891. He worked for the Young Men's Christian Association (YMCA), who wanted an indoor game to play during the cold winter months. Naismith nailed a peach basket high up at each end of the gym. Teams had to score by throwing a soccer ball into their basket – a peach would have been a bit messy! Nowadays, lightweight balls are used. Players "dribble" (bounce) them as they run.

THE BASKET
In 1906, hoops with open bottoms were introduced, to make it easier to retrieve the ball after a goal was scored. Modern hoops stand at 3.05 m (10 feet) high.

"MAGIC" JOHNSON (b. 1959)
Earvin "Magic" Johnson had a huge following as the Los Angeles Lakers' star player and the most valuable basketball player ever. But in 1991, he retired from the game after discovering he was HIV positive. Since then, he has led campaigns about HIV and AIDS, and has encouraged young people to become involved in sports.

Johnson

A TALL ORDER
The taller you are, the closer you can get to the basketball hoop – so tall players are in great demand! Most players are over 1.8 m (6 feet) tall; some have been as tall as 2.4 m (8 feet)!

INSTANT SUCCESS

The first proper basketball game was played in January 1892, with seven men on each team. Team sizes later went up to nine, then decreased to eight. Eventually it was decided that a team of five was best. Basketball caught on straight away. Colleges and schools began to organise competitions and soon it was the most widely played team game in the USA. Exciting modern players, like the great Michael Jordan, have made sure that basketball has continued to be a popular game around the world.

VOLLEYBALL

Volleyball is another indoor sport invented by a YMCA teacher. In 1895, William Morgan devised the game, in which two teams of six players hit the ball over a high net with their raised hands. Today, over 150 countries are members of the International Volleyball Federation and it is an Olympic sport.

NETBALL

This seven-a-side game, based on basketball, was invented in the 1890s. It is played only by women. The method of scoring and goal height are similar to basketball, but the players are not allowed to run with the ball. Netball courts are slightly larger than basketball ones.

THAT'S ENTERTAINMENT!

The world's best-known basketball team is the Harlem Globetrotters, a professional team founded in 1927. The Globetrotters tour the world, playing exhibition games (rather than official contests) in front of huge crowds.

PLAYING ZONES

Netball players wear coloured vests showing their positions. The letters mean: K–keeper *(pictured)*; G–goal; W–wing; D–defence; C–centre; A–attack; S–shooter.

BATS AND BALLS

Hitting a ball with a club or bat has always been used as entertainment. Cricket and baseball attract a huge amount of support and excitement, but they are very different games.

The origin of cricket, *Creag*, was played in medieval Britain with a curved stick or shepherd's crook, called a *cryc*. Between the fifteenth and eighteenth centuries, people played "stool ball", named after the three-legged milking stools used as wickets. Sometimes players used several stools and the batsmen moved to a new one after each ball.

Baseball

Cricket

HAVING A BALL
Early cricket balls were wooden; today they are covered in leather (as are baseballs and softballs). Some bowlers can reach ball speeds of up to 170 km (105 miles) per hour. Many batters wear helmets, because a hard cricket ball can cause a serious injury.

— Leather

— Cork

Twine

INTERNATIONAL CONTESTS

By 1800, cricket was one of the only team games with rules. Fans enjoyed local matches, but the Test matches (international games) caused the most excitement. Missionaries, soldiers and traders spread cricket around the world. In 1883, when England won a Test match in Australia, the bails were burnt, so the regular match between the countries was nicknamed the Ashes. Other top international teams include South Africa, India, New Zealand, Pakistan, the West Indies and Sri Lanka.

WHAT A GENT!
Early nineteenth-century cricketers were known as "Gentlemen". They were not allowed to play for money and were expected to look smart at all times. "Gentlemen's" cricket teams continued to be a tradition until 1962.

Grace

W.G. GRACE (1848-1915)
William Gilbert Grace of England was a doctor – and a world-famous cricketer, too! He is believed to have scored nearly 80,000 runs during his career (1865-1908).

Bails

The wicket

Stumps

BASEBALL BATS
Modern bats are 1 m (3.3 feet) long. Most are made of aluminium, but many players prefer wood. People used to cheat by filling their bats with cork for extra bounce.

1720

1750

1900

1800

CRICKET BATS

The first cricket bats were curved. This was fine for hitting balls from traditional underarm bowling. But after the introduction of overarm, fast bowling, in the nineteenth century, straighter, heavier bats were developed.

HIT AND RUN

Batsmen try to protect the wicket *(see page 10)*; if the ball hits it, they are "out". They must get as many runs (reaching the bowler's end before the ball is returned to the wicket) as possible. A batsman who makes 100 runs scores a "century". The team with the most runs is the winner.

SERIOUS MESSAGES

Sport can often be used to combat prejudice. Albert Goodwill Spalding (1850-1915), a US baseball player, took teams around the world. He included black players in a tour of the southern US states, at a time when black players were banned.

BASEBALL CRAZY!

Every year, more than 150 million American fans attend baseball games and 10 million play baseball for leisure. At first, baseball was known as "American cricket", a term hated in the USA. But an inquiry in 1905 ruled that it had been invented in 1839 by New Yorker Abner Doubleday, who had never heard of cricket. The first baseball team, the Knickerbocker Base Ball Club of New York, was formed in 1845. Baseball became popular with workers who only had half a day off a week – enough for a baseball game rather than a cricket match. Players like Babe Ruth (1895-1948, *right*) increased the game's popularity.

A GAME FOR THE BRAVE!

Hockey is played with a curved stick, or "hooky" *(above)*, from which it probably got its name. It is a hectic mixture of ancient games including Irish hurling, Scottish shinty and English bandy, although the ancient Greeks played a similar game 4,000 years ago. Hockey is also played on ice *(left)*, in a fast-moving, dangerous sport that is very popular in Canada and the USA.

RACKETS AND BALLS

"Real" or "royal" tennis, an indoor game, developed in the Middle Ages. The courts were walled stone yards divided by rope. Walter Wingfield of Britain invented lawn tennis in 1873, as a tonic for his wife. In 1877, the All-England Lawn Tennis and Croquet Club *(left)* in Wimbledon, London, held the first tennis tournament. This became "Wimbledon" – the world's most famous tennis competition. Improved training and playing techniques mean that the game is now fast-moving and exciting. International contests attract millions of viewers and the top players are superstars.

Badminton

QUICK AND LIGHT

A game similar to badminton was recorded in China over 2,000 years ago. In the nineteenth century, British officials in India learnt a shuttlecock game

called *poona*, which they took back to Britain. It was given the name "badminton" after the Duke of Beaufort played it at his home, Badminton House. Badminton players use shuttlecocks instead of a ball. Originally these were made of cork with a crown of goose feathers; modern ones are plastic.

Squash

A HIGH-SPEED SPORT
The fastest recorded tennis serve by a man is 222 km (138 miles) per hour, by Steve Denton of the USA in 1984. Both Jana Novotna of the Czech Republic and Brenda Schultz of the Netherlands broke the women's record in 1993, with a speed of 185 km (115 miles) per hour.

FAST AND FURIOUS

Squash is another racket sport, but it uses a softer, faster ball. The game is thought to have been invented in the yard of the notorious Fleet Debtors' Prison, London, in the seventeenth century. Players try to hit the ball against a wall so that their opponent will not be able to return it.

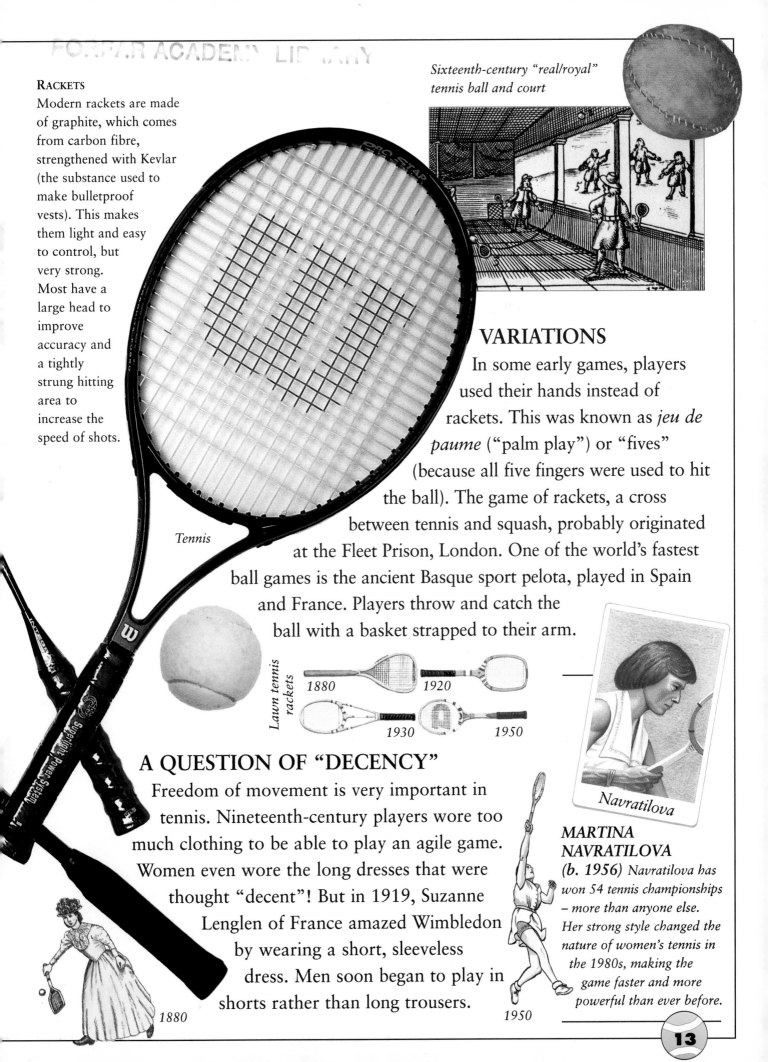

RACKETS

Modern rackets are made of graphite, which comes from carbon fibre, strengthened with Kevlar (the substance used to make bulletproof vests). This makes them light and easy to control, but very strong. Most have a large head to improve accuracy and a tightly strung hitting area to increase the speed of shots.

Tennis

Sixteenth-century "real/royal" tennis ball and court

VARIATIONS

In some early games, players used their hands instead of rackets. This was known as *jeu de paume* ("palm play") or "fives" (because all five fingers were used to hit the ball). The game of rackets, a cross between tennis and squash, probably originated at the Fleet Prison, London. One of the world's fastest ball games is the ancient Basque sport pelota, played in Spain and France. Players throw and catch the ball with a basket strapped to their arm.

Lawn tennis rackets

1880   1920

1930   1950

Navratilova

MARTINA NAVRATILOVA

(b. 1956) *Navratilova has won 54 tennis championships – more than anyone else. Her strong style changed the nature of women's tennis in the 1980s, making the game faster and more powerful than ever before.*

A QUESTION OF "DECENCY"

Freedom of movement is very important in tennis. Nineteenth-century players wore too much clothing to be able to play an agile game. Women even wore the long dresses that were thought "decent"! But in 1919, Suzanne Lenglen of France amazed Wimbledon by wearing a short, sleeveless dress. Men soon began to play in shorts rather than long trousers.

1880

1950

GOLF

In the fourteenth century, *kolf,* a game with a stick and a ball, was widely played in the Netherlands. This was probably the first kind of golf. Shortly afterwards, bandy ball *(see below)* was invented in England.

Modern golf originated in Scotland in the fifteenth century, from where it was taken to Europe by King James VI (James I of Britain). The first golf club, Saint Andrew's in Scotland, was founded in 1754. Women began to play golf in the nineteenth century, and it soon became equally popular among men and women.

THE HASKELL BALL
In 1902, Coburn Haskell invented a ball made of rubber strips wound around a rubber core, a design that is still used today. The dimples on the ball increase the distance and accuracy of its flight.

WOODS
Different golf clubs are used for different shots. Woods, which are designed to hit the ball for long distances, are made of wood – or plastic, graphite or metal!

IRONS
There are ten different types of iron, designed to give the ball height.

LOOK OUT!
Early golfers wore a red coat or shirt *(below)*, to avoid hitting each other with the balls. Today, players shout "fore!" as they make a shot, to warn other people on the course.

JOIN THE CLUB

By the end of the nineteenth century, modern golf was popular throughout Europe and Scottish emigrants had taken the game to the USA and other countries. Golf was mainly popular among wealthy people, because they had the time to spend whole days playing and because club membership and golf equipment were expensive. Unfortunately, this is still true today. Modern golf courses are carefully designed and maintained, and there are thousands worldwide, with new ones opening every day. The longest course is the massive International Golf Club in Massachusetts, USA. Players have to travel a staggering 7,612 m (25,200 feet) to play its eighteen holes!

BANDY BALL
The game that seems closest to golf is bandy ball *(above)*, played in sixteenth-century England, but it was probably more like hockey. Players used curved sticks to hit a ball into a goal.

Tee   *Rough*   *Fairway*

WEDGES
These are needed when the ball lands in a sand bunker (ditch). The player uses a wedge to "chip" the ball up and over the edge of the bunker.

PUTTERS
These are flat-ended clubs for rolling the ball over short distances onto the green (where the hole is located).

THE GENTEEL SPORT
Croquet *(right)*, in which players use a long mallet to hit a wooden ball through a series of hoops, originated in Ireland in the early 1800s and soon became a very popular garden game. Today, croquet is played as an organised sport in South Africa, New Zealand, the USA, Australia and Britain.

COMPETITIVE PLAY
Golf competitions are now very important. Every two years since 1927, professional golf players in the USA and Britain have played in the Ryder Cup competition. A European team replaced Britain in 1979. Top golf players can earn huge amounts of money for winning a contest – sometimes as much as £250,000 – and through sponsorship deals from various companies.

WHAT TO WEAR
Early players wore smart, formal outfits, but since the 1930s people have worn much more casual clothes. Modern golfers wear brightly pattered jumpers and trousers and a sunshade or cap to keep the sun out of their eyes. They wear a glove on their left hand to help them grip the club firmly, and special shoes *(left)* to stop their feet from slipping while they take their shots. Professional golfers usually display sponsors' names on their clothes.

JOYCE WETHERED
(b. 1901) Wethered is regarded as one of the best golfers ever. In five English Ladies' Championships in a row, she played 33 matches – and won every single one. She made similar achievements in many other contests. Her amazing power and accuracy revolutionised women's golf.

Wethered

THE COURSE
Most golf courses have 18 holes, with obstacles such as bunkers, water-filled ditches and trees.

Players have to hit the ball into each hole. The winner is the player who completes the course by taking the fewest strokes at the ball.

Green   Pin (hole)

Bunker

WINTER SPORTS

The earliest record of skiing is a 4,000-year-old painting of a skier in a Norwegian cave. Originally, skis were used for transport *(left)* and were improved by Scandinavian armies over the centuries. Skiing for pleasure began in the 1800s. Skiing holidays became popular in the 1920s, when Swiss and Austrian Alpine villages developed into ski resorts. Other resorts were later built in France, Italy and the USA, by blasting the mountainside to make ski tracks *(pistes)*. Snowboarding *(see page 17)* is now a fast-growing sport.

THE MODERN SKI

The basic shape of skis has stayed the same for at least 4,000 years. A ski is designed to work as an extension of the foot. Early skis were wooden, but modern ones are made of plastic, fibreglass and alloy metals. To help the skier stop or turn, they have steel edges which cut into the snow. Ski boots *(right)* are high-sided and stiff, to hold the leg in the right position and to protect the ankle.

DOWNHILL RACERS

Many people simply enjoy skiing as part of their winter holiday, but competitive skiing is a major sport. Alpine competitive skiing began in 1922 *(left)* when Arnold Lunn invented rules for downhill racing, in which skiers race straight down a slope, and slalom (zig-zag) racing around posts. These were later accepted as Olympic sports. Since 1967, an annual World Cup competition has also been held. Competitive skiing is very demanding and skiers must be extremely fit, in order to avoid serious injury.

SLINKY SUITS
Streamlined clothing lets skiers reach higher speeds. Most wear a Lycra (elastic) bodysuit, which reduces air resistance and keeps their muscles warm.

1500

1800

1900

1990

SPORTS ON ICE

Early skates were made from animal bones and used for transport. By the 1600s, Europeans were racing on frozen rivers, and skating contests began in the 1890s. Ice hockey *(see page 11)* is the most popular skating sport. Curling is played by teams of four, in Scotland, Canada and Scandinavia. It is like bowls on ice, using specially shaped stones. The players wear rubber-soled boots.

SPEEDY SKATERS
The first high-speed skating competitions took place in the Netherlands, where people raced each other on frozen canals in the seventeenth century. Modern racers use special, long-bladed speed skates and race against the clock rather than each other. Like skiers, they wear Lycra suits which cover their heads as well as their bodies *(above)*.

TOBOGGANS
The earliest known toboggan was used in Finland in 6500 BC. The name comes from the Native North American word for sledge, *tobakan*. These sledges were made of thin wood curled up at the front. Toboggan racing began in Switzerland in the 1880s. Today, bobsleds (or bobsleighs, *below*) reach incredibly high speeds.

Henie

SONJA HENIE (1912-69)
Henie became world famous as a skilful, exciting figure (artistic) skater. During her twelve-year career, she won 1,473 cups, medals and trophies, including three Olympic gold medals. She later became a successful Hollywood film star.

RIDING THE SNOWY WAVES

People are always looking for new thrills and speed in the snow. Snowboarding is a fast sport, invented by surfers who wanted to used their skills in the winter. Instead of skis, snowboarders use a single wide board *(right)*, like a surfboard, to perform jumps, twists and long downhill runs. Snowboarding will become an Olympic sport at the 1998 Winter Olympics in Japan.

LUGE AWAY!
Luge tobogganing is an Olympic sport. The luge is 1.5 m (5 feet) long and is steered by the feet and a rope. Modern competitors (one or two) lie on their back and descend feet first.

Early luge

17

WATER AND SPORT

Until the eighteenth century, it was widely believed that water spread diseases. But as swimming later became a popular leisure activity *(below)*, keen swimmers began to race one another. The first competition was held in London in 1837. The exploits of swimmers Matthew Webb and Gertrude Ederle *(see page 19)* made swimming popular – and it still is today. Competitive swimming *(right)* and diving, in teams and as individuals, are now major Olympic events.

OLYMPIC YACHTING
There are Olympic events for smaller yachts and dinghies, which race over a triangular course. All the boats in each class have the same design, so great skill is needed to win a race.

YACHTING

Yachting originated in the Netherlands (the word "yacht" comes from the Dutch *jacht*, or small vessel). In 1660, King Charles II of Britain was given a yacht by Dutch visitors; the sport then spread and by the 1800s was popular worldwide. In 1851, the US yacht *America* sailed across the Atlantic to race against British yachts. It won the Queen's Cup (renamed "America's Cup"). US yachts took the cup every year until *Australia II* won it in 1983; but the USA has won it back since then.

FASTER AND FASTER!
In 1896, the men's Olympic 100 m freestyle (front crawl) was won in 82.2 seconds. The current world record stands at 48.21 seconds! This improvement is due to better training techniques, making swimmers fitter.

MESSING ABOUT IN BOATS
During the 1920s and 1930s, many rich families bought a boat to use at the weekend *(above)*, while skiffs – affordable small boats – were raced by single rowers.

A LONG HISTORY

Canoeing was invented by the Inuit of Canada, who since ancient times have used kayaks, or canoes made from animal skins on a wooden frame. It became a competitive sport in the 1860s. Modern canoes also have a wooden frame, covered in plastic or rubber.

Kayak

Modern canoe

WATERSKIING
Waterskiers are pulled over the water by a motor-boat. In competition, they slalom race or jump over ramps to earn points.

Rowing *(above)*, with single, pairs or teams of rowers, became a competitive sport in schools and universities during the nineteenth century. It is still popular today.

MATTHEW WEBB (1848-83)

Captain Webb was the first person to swim the English Channel – over 37 km (22 miles) – taking 21 hours 45 minutes. He drowned trying to swim across the Niagara rapids. Gertrude Ederle from New York was the first woman to swim the Channel, in 1926.

Webb

TAKING THE PLUNGE

Diving has changed little since ancient times *(right)*. Modern springboard divers use a board 3 m (10 feet) above the water. They perform acrobatic moves and win marks for style and technique and for completing the dive successfully. SCUBA diving, invented in the 1940s for underwater exploration, is now a leisure activity rather than a competitive sport. Divers use portable breathing equipment.

LIFE'S A BEACH!
Pacific islanders were the first to surf, on wooden planks; it is popular in the USA, Australia and Hawaii. Windsurfing uses a fibreglass board with a sail.

HUMAN STRENGTH

People settled arguments with their fists long before anyone staged fights as entertainment. The Greeks *(left)*, Romans and Minoans used boxing to train soldiers. Bare-knuckle boxing was popular until 1867, when the Marquess of Queensberry, an English sportsman, drew up new rules, like wearing gloves and fighting in short rounds. Boxing is still a huge spectator sport. Matches take place between players of a similar weight.

DEADLY HANDS
Karate ("open hands") dates from seventeenth-century Japan. It is a form of unarmed fighting with incredible force and accuracy. Experts can break wood or bricks with a single blow from their bare hand.

THE ART OF SELF DEFENCE
Martial arts originated in Asian countries such as China and Japan in the Middle Ages. Judo (self defence), from the Japanese phrase *ju-jitsu*, or "gentle way", was developed by ancient Samurai warriors. It became an Olympic sport in 1964. Contestants wear coloured belts to show their grade. A black belt is the highest.

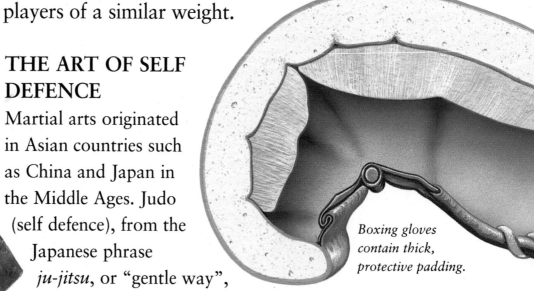

Boxing gloves contain thick, protective padding.

PURE POWER
Sumo has been a form of wrestling in Japan for over 700 years. The wrestlers try to push each other out of a circle.

PUMPING IRON
Weightlifting was a popular attraction at eighteenth and nineteenth-century fairs and circuses, and "strongmen" such as Eugene Sandow (1867-1925) became celebrities. It became a sport in the 1850s and the first world championship was held in 1891. It is now an Olympic event. Lifting weights is also a way of building up the muscle strength needed for many other sports.

MUSCLE POWER

Wrestling is as old as fist-fighting. Wrestlers competed at the first ancient Olympic Games, in 776 BC. There are many types of wrestling, but Graeco-Roman wrestling is the most well known. Together with freestyle, in which people use their legs as well as their arms, it is an Olympic sport. Other forms include: Yagli, the national sport of Turkey; Glima in Iceland; Cornish wrestling in England; and the wrestling at the Scottish Highland Games in which contestants grab each other's collar and elbow.

The annual Highland Games include many feats of strength, such as tossing the caber *(above)*, in which competitors must throw a whole tree trunk.

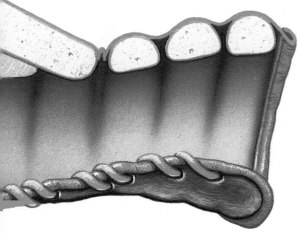

JOHN L. SULLIVAN (1858-1918)
Sullivan, a US bare-knuckle prizefighter, liked to boast that he could "lick any man in the world". During his career, he knocked out fifty challengers in a row and earned the nickname "the Boston Strong Boy". Sullivan won the world heavyweight boxing championship every year between 1882 and 1892.

Sullivan

MODERN FEATS OF STRENGTH

The spectacle of bodybuilding contests, in which competitors win points for the amount of muscle they have built up *(left)*, is a twentieth-century invention. This emphasis on muscle, however, has led to a worrying modern problem – the use of drugs by some athletes to build

Gladiator!
Television's *Gladiators* *(right)* take their name from the fighters of ancient Rome, but they compete only for fun – not to the death!

up their muscle tone and improve their performance. Anyone found to use drugs is punished severely.

ANIMALS AND SPORT

Humans have always used animals for food, entertainment and sport, from Minoan bull-leaping to royal hunting parties. The animals have had no choice! In many cultures, good hunters were believed to make successful leaders. Today, hunting is mainly done for sport, but many people say it is cruel and should be banned. Other sports that cause pain to animals, like dog and cock fighting, are illegal in many places.

The horse has always been the most valued animal in sport, whether for hunting or racing. Horses are still used in the ancient game of polo, in showjumping and racing and at US rodeos.

ANCIENT CHARIOTS
The ancient Egyptians enjoyed chariot racing *(above)* as long ago as 1200 BC and it was described by the ancient Greek poet Homer. Harness racing, a modern version, is still popular. The horses trot while the rider sits in a two-wheeled "sulky" (cart).

THE ROYAL SPORT

Flat racing, known as "the sport of kings" because it was liked by English rulers, spread after the thirteenth century. Steeplechasing (racing over fences) began in Ireland, where legend says that two riders raced over fields and bushes to reach a church. Races and race horses are now worth huge amounts of money.

A TEST OF SKILL
In showjumping, horses must jump over fences around a short course *(see page 23)*. This also forms part of three-day eventing (horse trials), in which riders must show their skill at handling their horse. The other events in horse trials are dressage (tightly controlled exercises) and a cross country trial over a 16-km (9.6-mile) course.

A MOST HISTORIC RACE
The *Siena Palio,* a summer race held in Siena, Italy, still follows rules drawn up in 1659. Horses from each of the 17 city districts race three times around the city square.

AN EXCLUSIVE GAME

The sport of polo is probably older than horse racing. The Persians played it over 4,000 years ago, and archaeologists in China have found 1,000-year-old murals of women playing the game, which they called *pulu* (the name of the willow root used to make the balls). It is still played, but it is not very widespread because polo ponies are expensive to buy, rear and train.

THE COURSE
Showjumping obstacles may be banks, hedges and water-filled ditches, or specially made fences, bars *(below)*, gates and walls. These may be combined to make more complicated jumps. Riders must complete a course within a certain time, trying not to knock down any of the jumps.

THE RULES OF POLO
Polo is played by two teams of four riders. They try to hit the ball into their opponents' goal, using long wooden mallets.

ICE DOGS

For thousands of years, husky dogs have been used by Inuit peoples for hunting and travelling, because they can pull sleds rapidly over ice and snow and are easy to care for and feed. Nowadays, large dogsled teams compete annually in a gruelling 1,936-km (1,159-mile) race across Alaska, which takes at least ten days.

IT'S A DOG'S LIFE
Other types of dog are specially bred and trained for racing. Thousands of years ago, greyhounds were used for hunting foxes and deer. Today, many of these fast-moving, long-legged dogs are made to race around a track, chasing a fake hare fixed on metal runners.

Red Rum

RED RUM (1965-95) *Red Rum was one of the fastest horses ever. He won the British Grand National steeplechase three times and came second twice – a racing record. He is buried under the Grand National's finishing post as a tribute to his success.*

FIELD EVENTS

Field events are athletics competitions which involve jumping or throwing. Many of these sports, such as discus-throwing, were an important part of life in ancient Greece and Rome and were a main feature of the early Olympic Games. The Roman emperor Theodosius banned the Games in AD 393, but the events were passed down through time. Many other field events were invented in Scotland over the centuries, and became part of the modern Olympics.

THE EARLY ATHLETES

The word "athletics" comes from the ancient Greek word *athlos*, or fight. Ancient Greek athletes were always male and competed naked – women were not allowed to watch competitions. The Greek Olympics were held in honour of the god Zeus. Discus throwing *(above)*, which featured in the ancient Olympic Games, may have had its origins in the flat, round shields used by Greek soldiers, for whom athletics were an important part of their military training.

UP 'N' OVER!

Pole vaulting originated in Scotland hundreds of years ago and is one of the oldest field events. It was invented to help people jump walls and ditches. The original wooden poles were replaced in the early twentieth century by bamboo ones. Since the 1950s, carbon fibre poles have been used because of their lightness and strength. In 1896, the record vault height was 3.3 m (11 feet); today, it is over 6 m (20 feet).

POLE VAULT

Pole vaulters prepare for a jump by taking a long run towards the crossbar. They plant the end of the pole in a take-off box so that the pole bends. As it straightens, it provides the power to lift them upwards towards the crossbar. They then twist their body so that it goes over the bar, and fall backwards onto thick matting beneath.

Javelin

Shot

Pole vault

Discus

Long/triple jump

TAKE A RUNNING JUMP!

The only jumping event in the ancient Olympics was the long jump *(below)*. The triple jump and high jump began at the Highland Games. Triple jumpers need great strength. They must take a hop and a step and then jump as far as possible. Until 1968, high jumpers simply swung their legs over the bar. Then Dick Fosbury of the USA reached new heights by flopping backwards over it – and invented the Fosbury Flop!

FANCY FOOTWEAR
High-jump shoes are designed to provide firm contact with the ground, to increase the athlete's accuracy. They have up to 11 spikes.

GOOD SHOT!

A shot is a smooth, heavy ball made of brass or iron *(right)*. In the original event, which was invented in medieval Scotland, heavy stones or cannon balls were used. The modern shot weighs 7.3 kg (16.06 lb) for men and 3.6 kg (7.92 lb) for women, and must be thrown as far as possible from within a 2.1-m (7-foot) circle. Current champions can reach distances of about 23 m (76 feet) for men and 22 m (73 feet) for women.

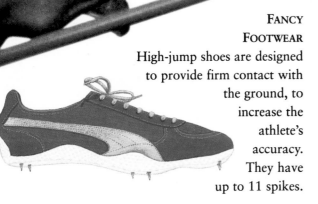

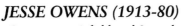

JESSE OWENS (1913-80)
Owens won 1 field and 3 track gold medals for the USA at the 1936 Berlin Olympics, but the Nazi dictator Hitler would not applaud him. Owens was a hero, both for his athletics (he broke 7 world records) and for his campaigns against racism.

Owens

THE SPACE RACE
Spears have always been used worldwide, for hunting and for war. Modern competition javelins are made with carbon fibre developed from the NASA space programme. The fibre is wrapped around a steel core then baked in a special oven at a computer-controlled temperature.

TRACK EVENTS

Track competitions include running and walking races. Both the ancient Greeks and Romans held running races, and various types of race have been popular ever since. Marathons, or long-distance road races, have mythical origins. One Greek legend tells of a messenger, Pheidippides, who ran 43 km (26 miles) from Marathon to Athens with news of a great victory – then died of exhaustion! This distance is still used for modern marathons. Race walking also covers long distances – up to 50 km (30 miles). Walkers try to reach a speed of 15 km (9 miles) per hour.

Running track

THE IMPORTANCE OF TIME
Before stopwatches were invented, there was no proper timing of races and competitors simply raced against each other.

Clockwork watches have now been replaced by electronic timers which can read times to thousandths of a second *(left)*. This is vital when a split second can make the difference between winning or losing, or can set a new record.

A CHALLENGING EVENT
Hurdling *(below)* became a competitive event in the 1870s. The idea came from cross-country running, which often involved jumping over fences and hedges. Ten hurdles must be cleared in as short a time as possible.

ON YOUR MARKS...
The 100-m sprint is one of the fastest, most exciting races of all. The sprinters start from special blocks *(left)* so that they can take off easily and reach a high speed in a short time.

EDUCATED ATHLETES
Nineteenth-century English schools and colleges invented various forms of cross-country running *(right)*. Paper chases were led by a single runner who scattered a trail of paper – but the sport was stopped by an anti-litter law! Cross-country running is still a popular sport both for amateur and professional athletes.

THE SPIRIT OF THE OLYMPICS

The modern Olympics were first held in 1896 to promote world peace. The rings on the flag represent the five continents, linked in friendship, and at least one of the colours is shown on every flag in the world. New sports, like synchronised swimming and snowboarding, feature in the Olympics every year, but the Games still include events with ancient origins, such as gymnastics.

SPORT FOR ALL

Disability does not prevent athletes from taking part in all events. The Paralympics for disabled sportspeople are held every four years, while athletes with disabilities have competed and won medals in the Olympics and the Commonwealth Games. Athletes in wheelchairs compete in all the major marathons.

WOMEN'S GYMNASTICS

This became an Olympic event in 1952. Only women perform on the beam (right) and asymmetrical bars. For decades, Russian gymnasts have dominated all the major competitions.

MEN'S GYMNASTICS

Men's gymnastics became an Olympic event in 1900. Only men perform on the parallel and horizontal bars, rings and pommel horse (above).

THE LIFE OF A CHAMPION

Gymnastics requires a huge amount of training and great physical strength. Gymnasts, like all athletes, must devote themselves to their sport.

OLGA KORBUT (b. 1956)

Seventeen year-old Korbut, from the former USSR, shot to fame with her brilliant performance at the 1972 Olympic Games. She was loved by the public for her breathtaking gymnastic skills and warm personality. Her fame greatly increased the worldwide popularity of gymnastics.

SPIETH

Korbut

CYCLE SPORTS

In 1690, Monsieur de Sivrac of France showed off a machine made from two wooden wheels joined by a crossbar. The rider moved it by pushing with his or her feet. The pedal cycle was invented in 1840. Early cycles *(right)* had a big front wheel and a small back one and were called "penny farthings" after large and small British coins. Cycles with same-sized wheels were invented in the 1880s. Today, cycle races are held both on tracks and on roads.

STREAMLINING

Racing bikes have solid wheels *(right)*, because spokes *(top)* catch the air and increase air resistance, so reducing the speed. To further increase their speed, riders wear streamlined polyester helmets.

FROM BONESHAKER TO BMX
Early bicycles were uncomfortable and hard to ride, with no gears to make cycling easier. Modern mountain bikes have over 20 gears. In 1984, Nicholas and Richard Crane cycled up Kilimanjaro, the highest mountain in Africa, on their mountain bikes!

TREADS AND TYRES
Early cycle wheels had solid rubber tyres. In 1887, the Scottish inventor John Dunlop developed an air-filled (pneumatic) tyre to help his child win a tricycle race. These tyres made speed cycle racing possible. They have been used on cycles and cars ever since.

IN PURSUIT OF THE YELLOW JERSEY

Organised cycle racing began in France in 1868. The Tour de France *(right)*, the world's most gruelling road race, was first held there in 1903. For three weeks, riders race for 5,000 km (3,000 miles) through France – including a climb into the Alps! Over ten million people watch the race on TV.

COMBINED EVENTS

The toughest competitions are the combined events, in which athletes must succeed in various sports: **decathlon** (men only) – 100-m sprint, long jump, shot, high jump, 400 m, 110 m hurdles, discus, pole vault, javelin, 1,500 m; **heptathlon** (women only) – 100 m hurdles, shot, high jump, 200 m, long jump, javelin, 800 m; **modern pentathlon** (men only) –

horseback riding, fencing, pistol shooting, swimming, cross-country running; **triathlon** – 3.8 km sea swimming, 180 km cycling, 42.2 km marathon running; **biathlon** – cross-country skiing over 10 and 20 km (men) or 5 and 10 km (women), with rifle shooting at certain points *(above left)*. Australian life guards compete in "Iron Man" combined events *(above)*.

SWORD PLAY

HI-TECH CONTESTS
Modern fencers wear clothing that is electronically wired, to accurately register and record any successful hits from their opponent.

Fencing is part of the modern pentathlon as well as being an individual Olympic contest. In the Middle Ages, men spent many hours practising their sword skills and often settled arguments with duels. After the 1500s, the rapier – a slim, double-edged sword – was the most common weapon *(below)*. Rapier fighting (fencing) became a popular sport and was included in the 1896 Olympics. Women first competed in 1924.

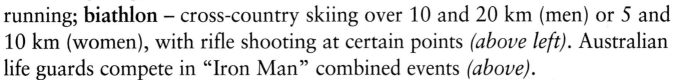

Thompson

DALEY THOMPSON (b. 1958) *Thompson is a British decathlete. He broke the world record four times and was the first athlete in the world to hold the Olympic, World, Commonwealth and European decathlon titles.*

SHOOTING EVENTS
Competitive shooting uses various types of weapon, including pistols and rifles. Competitors fire at both fixed and moving targets.

GAZETTEER

✹ indicates Olympic sports.
Page numbers are in brackets.

American Football (6) The first rules were drawn up in 1867. It involves much physical contact and is one of the most dangerous games played.

Archery ✹ First used for hunting; now a sport.

Athletics ✹ (26-28) Ancient running, jumping and throwing events.

Australian Rules football (7) Based on Gaelic football, it was first played in Australia in the 1860s.

Badminton ✹ (12) An ancient game, given its English name in the 1800s.

Bandy ball (11, 14) A medieval, hockey-like game.

Baseball (11) The USA's national summer game, first played in 1839.

Basketball ✹ (8) Teams throw the ball through a hoop. Invented in 1891.

Basque pelota (13) A Spanish and French game. Players use a basket to throw the ball.

Billiards A table game invented in fifteenth-century France.

Bobsledding ✹ (17) A sled with a small crew races against the clock. It became popular in Switzerland in the late nineteenth century.

Boules (petanque) A French ball game rather like bowls, first played in 1910.

Bowls A large ball is rolled to hit skittles or a smaller ball. Popular in third-century Germany then spread to Europe and the USA.

Boxing ✹ (20) After centuries of bare-knuckle fighting, the Queensberry Rules, 1867, imposed controls.

Bullfighting Spain's oldest national sport. Many people say that it is a cruel blood sport and should be banned.

Canoeing ✹ (19) An ancient Inuit tradition. Became a popular sport in the 1860s. Events include slalom and races against the clock.

Combined events ✹ (29) Athletes take part in a variety of sports. Some combinations are based on ancient methods of military training.

Commonwealth Games (27) Started in 1930 as the Empire Games, they take place every four years. Teams come from the countries once governed by Britain (the "Commonwealth").

Cricket (10-11) The English national summer sport. International (Test) matches are also played.

Croquet (15) A nineteenth-century garden game, based on golf.

Curling (17) A sport played on ice in Canada, Scotland and Scandinavia. Teams try to slide a stone across the ice so that it comes as close as possible to a target.

Cycling ✹ (28) Events include road, track and speedway racing. The biggest race is the Tour de France, first held in 1903.

Decathlon ✹ (29) Ten athletic events – four track and six field – over a two-day period. It is contested by male athletes only.

Diving ✹ (18) Includes springboard diving and platform diving from a rigid board. Points are awarded for skill and technique.

Equestrianism ✹ (22, 23) The sport of competitive riding, which includes show jumping, dressage, horse trials and carriage driving.

Fencing ✹ (29) Fighting with thin swords, part of the first modern Olympics. Fencers wear masks and protective jackets, wired to record hits.

Fives (13) A handball game for two or four players, first played at Eton School, England, in 1825 and based on earlier French games.

Gaelic Football (7) An Irish mixture of rugby and soccer. The annual All-Ireland Championship was first played in 1887.

Golf (14-15) Originated in the Netherlands. Players must hit a ball into 18 holes with as few strokes as possible.

Greyhound racing (23) Dogs race round a circuit, chasing a fake hare.

Gymnastics ✹ (27) Takes its name from the ancient Greeks. Gymnasts perform a variety of physical exercises using gym equipment.

Heptathlon ✹ (29) A combined event for women. It is held over 2 days and involves 7 different events.

Highland Games (21, 24, 25) Scottish summer contests which have changed little since ancient times.

Hockey ✹ (11) Played on grass, using sticks to hit a ball into a goal.

Horse racing (22, 23) Flat racing has a flat course; steeplechasing has fences. Harness racing uses "sulkies" (carts). Races have been held since the 1500s.

Hurling (11) An Irish team game using curved sticks and a ball. It was invented over 2,000 years ago.

Husky racing (23) Based on Inuit traditions, dog-pulled sledges race each other.

Ice hockey ✯ (11, 17) Uses a puck (rubber disc); popular in Canada, USA and Russia.

Judo ✯ (20) Japanese unarmed combat based on *ju-jitsu* ("gentle way").

Karate (20) A Japanese form of unarmed combat from the 1600s.

Lacrosse A team game invented by Native North American peoples, in which long-handled sticks are used to catch and throw a ball into the other team's goal.

Luge ✯ (17) High-speed racing against the clock on a one or two-person sled. It became a Winter Olympic event in 1964.

Marathon ✯ (26) A long-distance race invented in ancient Greece. Run over 26 miles 385 yards (about 43 km), it has been an Olympic event since 1896.

Motor cycling Motor-cross, speedway and road racing. Scandinavian speedway races are held on ice.

Motor racing Began in the early days of the car. Grand Prix races decide the Formula 1 World Champion every year.

Netball (9) A women's team game similar to basketball, invented in the 1890s.

Olympic Games First held in 776 BC near Olympia, Greece; banned in AD 394. The modern Games began in Athens, Greece, in 1896. Held every four years. The winter Games are held two years after the summer ones.

Pigeon fancying People have trained and raced pigeons since the 1300s.

Polo (23) Played on horseback. Invented in Persia over 4,000 years ago.

Pool A US table game with 15 balls which must be "potted" in a certain order.

Rackets (13) A tennis-like game played in an indoor, walled court; invented in the Middle Ages.

"Real/royal" tennis (12, 13) An indoor game, based on medieval French handball.

Road walking ✯ (26) Racers walk as fast as they can. The Lugano Trophy was first held in 1961.

Rowing ✯ (19) An ancient sport, first organised in the early 1800s. Boats hold up to 8 crew members.

Rugby (6, 7) Played with an oval ball. There are 2 forms, League and Union, with different rules. Both began in the nineteenth century.

Running ✯ (26) Races have taken place for centuries. Outdoor track races range from 100 m to 10,000 m in length. Cross-country courses are up to 12.5 km (7.5 miles) long.

SCUBA (19) Self-Contained Underwater Breathing Apparatus (1943).

Shinty (11) Invented in Ireland 1,500 years ago. A ball is hit with sticks.

Shooting ✯ (29) A sport since the 1400s, with still or moving targets.

Skating ✯ (17) An ancient means of transport. Events include figure skating and ice dancing. Speed skaters race against the clock or each other.

Skiing ✯ (16) A sport since 1924, but skis used for centuries.

Snooker Invented in 1875 by British soldiers in India.

Snowboarding ✯ (16, 17) An Olympic event after 1998.

Soccer (4-5) ★ Originated in the Middle Ages. The modern game developed in the nineteenth century

Squash (12) Probably invented in the Fleet Prison.

Sumo (20) A Japanese contest. Wrestlers try to push each other out of a circle.

Surfing (19) Riding waves on a board. Has an annual World Championship.

Swimming ✯ (18) A sport since the 1800s. Synchronised swimming is a new Olympic event.

Table tennis ✯ Based on lawn tennis.

Tennis ✯ (lawn tennis, 12, 13) It was invented in 1873 as a tonic.

Volleyball ✯ (9) Hitting a ball by hand over a net; started in the USA in 1895.

Water polo ✯ A football-like game played in a pool.

Waterskiing (19) Skiing on water behind a motor-boat.

Weightlifting ✯ (20) Began at early fairs and circuses.

Windsurfing ✯ (19) A form of surfing, with a sail.

Wrestling ✯ (21) An ancient sport. Fighters try to throw each other down.

Yachting ✯ (18) Became popular under Charles II.

INDEX

(More references may be found in the Gazetteer, pages 30-31.)

Ashes, the 10
Astro Turf 5
athletics 24-26
Aztecs 8

balls 10, 12, 14
bare-knuckle fighting 20, 21
bats 10, 11
Beaufort, Duke of 12
bicycles 28
bull-leaping 22

caber-tossing 21
chariots 22
China, ancient 4, 12
clothing 5, 10, 13, 14, 15, 16, 17, 20, 28,
courts 9, 12
Crane, Nicholas and Richard 28
Creag 10
cups
  America's 18
  Ryder 15
  World (rugby) 7
  World (skiing) 16
  World (soccer) 5, 16

Denton, Steve 12
Doubleday, Abner 11
drug abuse 3, 21
Dunlop, John 28

Ederle, Gertrude 18, 19
Egypt, ancient 22

Fleet Prison 12, 13
footwear 4, 5, 15, 16, 17, 25
Fosbury, Dick 25

"Gentlemen" 10
gladiators 21
Glima 21

goals 5, 8
golf clubs 14, 15
golf courses 15
Grace, W. G. 10
Grand National 23
Greece, ancient 11, 20, 24
greyhounds 23
guns 29

Harlem Globetrotters 9
Harpastum 4
Haskell, Coburn 14
Henie, Sonja 17
horses 22, 23
hunting 22, 23
huskies 23

Inuit 19, 23
"Iron Man" 29

Johnson, "Magic" 8
jeu de paume 13
ju-jitsu 20

kayaks 19
kolf 14
Korbut, Olga 27

Lenglen, Suzanne 13
Lockhart, Robert 14
Lomu, Jonah 7
Lunn, Arnold 16

Macmillan, Kirkpatrick 28
Maya 8
Minoans 20, 22
"mob football" 4
Morgan, William 9

Naismith, James 8
Navratilova, Martina 13
Novotna, Jana 12

Olympic Games 3, 16, 17, 18, 19, 20, 21, 24, 25, 27, 31
Owens, Jesse 25

Paganica 4

Pelé 5
Persia, ancient 23
pitches 5
pole vaulting 24
politics 3, 11, 25
poona 12
Pot-ta-Pok 8
protection
  body 6, 16, 21
  hands 21
  head 6, 7, 10, 28

Queensberry, Marquess of 20

Red Rum 23
referees 5
Romans 4, 20, 21
Roosevelt, Theodore 6
rules
  American football 6
  boxing 20, 30
  netball 9
  rugby 7
  skiing 16
  soccer 5
Ruth, Babe 11

Samurai warriors 20
Sandow, Eugene 20
Schultz, Brenda 12
shot 25
shuttlecocks 12
Sienna Palio 22
skiffs 18
ski resorts 16
Spalding, Albert Goodwill 11
speed
  of bowling 10
  of swimming 18
  of tennis serves 12
sponsorship 5, 15
"stool ball" 10
Sullivan, John 21
swords 29

Test matches 10
Theodosius 24
Thompson, Daley 29
timers 26
tlatchi 8

toboggans 17
Tour de France 28
Tsu-Chu-Tsu 4

waterskiing 19
Webb, Matthew 18, 19
Webb Ellis, William 7
Wethered, Joyce 15
wickets 10, 11
Wimbledon 12-13

Yagli 21
YMCA 8, 9

☆

Picture Credits
(t-top, m-middle, b-bottom, r-right, l-left):
3 all, 4-5mb, 8tr, 10b, 10-11, 11br, 12-13m, 14-15, 16ml & mr, 26ml, 32 – Roger Vlitos; Front cover tr, mm, bl & br 4t, 6b, 8b, 9t, 12m, 17t, 18tr, 19t, 20t & bl, 21t & bl, 22-23, 23t, 24b, 24-25, 25m, 27m, 27bl & br, 28b, 29tl & bl – Frank Spooner Pictures; Front cover ttl, ttm, tr, ml & mr, 4b, 11bl, 13t, 14b, 15tr, 16b, 20br, 25t, 26b, 27t, 28ml, 29br back cover centre – Mary Evans Picture Library; 4-5mt – Adidas UK Ltd; 5b, 6tr, 8tl, l0t – Spalding Sports Worldwide; 6tl – Schutt Sports; 7 both, 9b, 12t, 17b, 18bl, 18-19, 21br, 26mr, 28mr, 29tr – Rex Features; Front cover tm, 11m, 18tl & br, 22m, 28tl & tr – Hulton Getty Collection; 12-13t – Carlton Sports Company; 12-13b – Dunlop Slazenger; 19m, 22t – Ancient Art & Architecture Collection.
Special thanks to: Harrods, London; Cobra Golf Equipment; Grays Sports; Nordica Skiing Equipment; Salomon Skiing Equipment; Saxon Sports Timing; R.D. Paton Artificial Sports Surfaces.